Faith Inspired Obedience

So Much Better Than The Guilt And Reward System Of The Law!

Rudi Louw

Table of Contents

The Marvel of the Holy Bible

1. Uninterrupted Theme and Inspired Thought

It took *1,500 years* to compile the Holy Bible, involving *more than 40 different authors*. <u>Yet</u> the theme and inspired thought of Scripture continues *uninterrupted* from author to author, from beginning till end.

2. Absence of Mythical Stories

Compare philosophies and theories about creation in the Middle East, Europe, Asia, Africa, and Latin America and you'll find mythical scenarios: gods feuding and cutting up other gods to form the heavens and the earth, etc.

In ancient Greek mythology, the Greeks see Atlas carrying the earth on his shoulders. In India, Hindus believe eight elephants carry the earth on their backs.

But in contrast, Job, the oldest book in the Holy Bible, declares that, *"God suspends the earth on nothing."* (Job 26:7)

This was said millennia before Isaac Newton discovered the invisible laws of gravity that delicately balance every planet and sun in its individual circuit.

Contrary to every other ancient attempt to give a creation account, *the Holy Bible pictures the creation of the earth in a very scientific manner.*

For example, in Genesis Chapter One, the continents are lifted from the seas, then vegetation is formed and later animal life, all reproducing *'according to its own kind'*, **thus recognizing the fixed genetic laws.** In addition, we have the bringing forth of man and woman, *all done by God in a dignified and proper manner, without mythological adornments.*

The balance or remainder of the Holy Bible follows suite.

*The narratives are **true historical documents**, faithfully reflecting society and culture **as history and archaeology would discover them thousands of years later.** Not only is the Holy Bible historically accurate, it is also reliable when it deals with scientifically proven subjects.*

It was never intended to be a textbook on history, science, mathematics, or medicine. *However, when its writers touch on these subjects, **they often state facts that scientific advancement would not reveal, or***

6

even consider, until thousands of years later.

While many have doubted the accuracy of the Holy Bible, time and continued research have consistently demonstrated that the Word of God is better informed than its critics.

3. Intactness

Of all the ancient works of substantial size, *the Holy Bible survives intact, against all odds and expectations.*

Compared with other ancient writings, the Holy Bible has more manuscripts as evidence to support it than any ten pieces of classical literature combined!

The plays of William Shakespeare, for instance, were written about four hundred years ago, after the invention of the printing press. Many of his original writings and words have been lost in numerous sections, *yet the Holy Bible's uncanny preservation has weathered thousands of years of wars, contradictions, persecutions, fires and invasions.*

Through the centuries Jewish scribes have preserved the Holy Bible's Old Covenant text, **such as no other manuscripts have ever been preserved. They kept tabs on every letter, syllable, word and paragraph.** *They* *continued from generation to generation to appoint and train special groups of men within their culture* **whose sole duty it was to preserve and transmit these documents with perfect accuracy and fidelity**.

Who ever bothered to count the letters, syllables, or words of Plato, Aristotle, or Seneca for that matter?

When it comes to the New Testament, the actual number of preserved manuscripts is so great that it becomes overwhelming. ***There are more than 5,680 Greek manuscripts, more than 10,000 Latin Vulgate manuscripts and at least 9,300 other versions. Further still, there exists an additional 25,000 manuscript copies of portions of the New Testament.*** **No other document of antiquity even begins to approach such numbers.**

The closest in comparison is Homer's Iliad, with only 643 manuscripts. The first complete work of Homer only dates back to the 13th century.

4. Unmatched Accuracy in Predictive Foretelling

The Holy Bible is unmatched in accuracy in predictive foretelling. .No other ancient work succeeds in this, or even begins to attempt this.

Other books such as the Koran, the Book of Mormon, and parts of the Veda claim divine inspiration; **but none of these books contain predictive foretelling.**

This one undeniable fact we know for certain: *While microscopic scrutiny would show up the imperfections, blemishes, and defects of any work of man, <u>it magnifies the beauties and perfection of God</u>. Just as every flower displays in accurate detail the reflection and perfection of beauty, <u>so does the Word of Truth when it is scrutinized</u>.*

Historian Philip Schaff wrote:

"Without money and weapons, Jesus the Christ conquered more millions than Alexander, Caesar, Mohammad, and Napoleon. Without science and learning, He (Jesus the Christ) shed more light on things human and divine than all philosophers and scholars combined. Without the eloquence of schools, He (Jesus the Christ) spoke such words of life as was never spoken before or since and produced effects which lie beyond the reach of orator or poet. Without writing a single line, He (Jesus the Christ) set more pens in motion and furnished themes for more sermons, orations, discussions, learned volumes, works of art, and songs of praise **than the whole army of great men of ancient and modern times combined.**" (*The Person of Christ*, p33. 1913)

Today, there are literally billions of Bibles in more than 2,000 languages.

Isn't it about time you find out what it really has to say?

Hey listen, the Holy Bible is all about Jesus, the Messiah, the Christ...

...and everything about Jesus Christ is really about YOU!!

Study Tips:

Read 2 Corinthians 5:14, 16, 18, 19, and 21.

In the light of these Scriptures, it should be obvious that, if you want to study the Holy Bible, *you should study it in the light of Mankind's redemption!*

Feed daily on **redemption realities** found in the book of Acts, in Romans Chapters One through Eight, and in Ephesians, Colossians, and Galatians. These realities are also found in 1 Peter Chapter One, 2 Peter Chapter One, James Chapter One, as well as in 1 and 2 Corinthians.

Acknowledgment

I want to acknowledge and thank one of my mentors in the faith, Francois du Toit, for blessing and impacting me with revelation knowledge.

I borrowed the portion on *"The Marvel of the Holy Bible"* from his website: http://www.MirrorWord.net, as students so often feel they have a right to do with things that come from teachers they respect. Just as Galatians 6:6 says, *"Let him who is taught the Word **share in all good things** with him who teaches."*

To all our dear friends and family, for all the love and support, and to Chase Aderhold and all those who helped me with this project:

THANK YOU!

Also, especially to my wife, Carmen;

For keeping me real by being my companion in life and partner in ministry,

I love and appreciate you so very much!

Foreword

Thank you for taking the time to read this book.

Let me start off by saying that *I am totally addicted to my Daddy's love for me.*

I am in love with Jesus Christ, *and that is enough for me!*

The love of God is so much more than a doctrine, a philosophy, or a theory. It is so much more and goes so much deeper than knowledge; it way surpasses knowledge. *We are talking heart language here.*

Thus, I write *to impact people's hearts,* to make them see the mysteries that have been hidden in Father God's heart concerning Christ Jesus, and actually *concerning THEM,* so as to arrest their conscience with it, *that I may introduce them to their original design and to their true selves,* **and present them to themselves perfect in Christ Jesus** *and set them apart unto Him* **in love***,* as a chaste virgin.

We are involved with the biggest romance of the ages.

Therefore this book cannot be read as you would a novel: *casually.* It is not a cleverly devised little myth or fable. **It contains** revelation and *truth* into some things you may or may not have considered before.

It is *the TRUTH of God, ultimate TRUTH, and therefore has direct bearing upon YOUR life.* The Word and the Spirit are my witness *to the reality of these things!*

Be like the people of Berea the apostle Paul ministered to in Acts 17:11. Open yourself up to study the revelation contained in this book *to discover for yourself the reality of these things*.

Be forewarned! Do not become guilty of the sins of the Pharisees, **or you too will miss out on the depth of fulfillment God Himself, who is LOVE, wants to give you**.

Jesus said of the Pharisees and Sadducees that they strain out every little gnat BUT swallow whole camels. What He meant by that is that *some people seem to have it all together when it comes to doctrine and they love to argue.* **It makes them feel important, but it is nothing other than EMPTY religious and intellectual pride.** *They know the Scriptures in and out, and YET they are still so IGNORANT about* **REAL TRUTH that is only found in LOVE.** *They are still so ignorant and indifferent* **towards the things that REALLY MATTER**. They are always arguing over the use of *every little jot and tittle* and over the meaning and interpretation of *every word of Scripture.*

The exact thing they accuse everyone else of doing though, the precise thing they judge everyone else for, *they are actually doing themselves.* That is **they often downright misinterpret and twist what is being said,** *making a big deal of insignificant things while obscuring or weakening God's real truth: the truth of His LOVE.* They are *always majoring on minors <u>because they do not understand the heart of God</u> and therefore they constantly miss the whole point of the message.*

Paul himself said it so beautifully,

*"...the letter kills but **the Spirit BRINGS LIFE;"***

*"...<u>knowledge puffs up</u>, but **LOVE EDIFIES**."*

I say again:

Allow yourself to get caught up in the revelation I am about to share. Open yourself up to study the insight contained in this book, *not only with a desire to gain knowledge, but also with anticipation **to hear from Father God yourself;***

*...**to encounter Him through His Word;***

*...**and to embrace truth, in order to know and believe the LOVE God has for <u>you</u>,** so that you may get so caught up in it, **that you too may receive from Him LOVES' impartation of LIFE.***

This revelation contains within it the voice and call of LOVE Himself to every human being on the face of this earth. *If you take heed to it, it is custom designed and guaranteed to forever alter and enrich your life*

Prayer

Thank you Father that we are not the product of our own effort,

…and neither is our relationship with You the product of our own effort.

Thank you Father that we are not the product of some religious mold, but we are Your workmanship; *Your one of a kind masterpiece!* We carry the very stamp of your approval in our spirits.

So Father we rejoice in You today, for You design and make all things well. Your work is perfect. And we thank you for it; for Your workmanship in us!

We ascribe unto You, greatness and glory and splendor, as we reflect back to You our joy and the abundant evidence of our gratitude, *for we truly enjoy every good thing that belongs to us in Christ Jesus.*

Thank you precious Father God.

We honor Your working in our lives; we treasure Your gospel and Your truth revealed in the New Testament *above all other wealth.*

We treasure Your Word revealed *above all other wealth.*

Thank you for Jesus!

Thank you for the ministry of Your Holy Spirit!

Thank you for revealing and giving even Yourself to us!

Thank you for loving us so very much, Father God.

Thank you for the living and abiding word of truth; *the living and abiding **Word.***

Thank you for each other! Thank you that You have made us for, and now given us as gifts, to one another.

In Jesus Name.

Amen!

Hallelujah!

"My mission,
through my ministry,
is **to bring about
the obedience <u>of</u> faith,**
for the sake of His name,
among all the nations."
- Paul (Romans 1:5)

"Thanks be to God that,
even though **you were once**
slaves of sin,
**yet you have become
obedient from the heart,**
to that **exact standard of**

teaching *delivered to you*
(or to which you were
delivered,
in other words:
by which you were delivered) "
~ (Romans 6:17)

"God is able
to **establish** *you*
by my gospel
which has to do with
the preaching of Jesus Christ,
according to the revelation
of the mystery

which has now been <u>made</u>
<u>manifest,</u>
and through the prophetic
Scriptures
has been made <u>known</u>
to all the nations,
according to the
commandment
(or persuasive and convincing
argument or, emphatic
statement or, endorsement,
and declaration;
revealed WORD, &
unveiled truth or,

reality revealed)
of the everlasting God
for the obedience <u>of</u> faith"
          - Romans 16:25-26

Chapter 1

Law Motivated Obedience

We have been having such a good time of fellowship here in our home lately, just indulging together in the Word and discovering afresh the foundation of God's approval of us.

It has been even better than what we have been enjoying in our meetings...

Well, almost... ha... ha... ha...

Even though our Sunday morning get together start somewhere between 10:30 and 10:45am, many times it has been almost 3:00pm before we can close the meeting.

Trust me when I say to you that what we have been enjoying both in our home and in our corporate meetings have been so tremendous and spectacular and wonderful that we are all just running over with joy in our enjoyment and encounter of God… ha… ha… ha…

It is this inspired fellowship around the eternal truth of redemption that has moved me to write all the books in this series on **helping the believer to fully appropriate truth, or *faith inspired ministry*.** In this particular book, I want us to consider the theme **Faith Inspired Obedience**.

If you haven't gotten the other books in this series, you should really get them and study them. I can personally guarantee that you will be impacted in your relationship with Father God and that there will come an expansion in your spirit through revelation knowledge and such a freshness in your encounter with God that it will launch your life and ministry to others into new and greater dimensions of impact than ever before.

Faith inspired obedience is a different kind of obedience than an obedience which is guilt or reward motivated.

You see the Law also motivates obedience.

Whether it is societal law in general, the Law of Moses, Islamic Law, or any other religious law or moral code, or merely the strong opinions of your parents or peers that govern and guide you, **the point is** *whatever law of conscience you try to live by,* ***through its promises of punishment and reward*** *the Law also motivates some kind of obedience.*

But you see, that obedience will limit you to your own effort, *to your own ability to obey.*

Most of the time under that law-system; that system of obligation, *you will find yourself under the dominion of guilt, shame and condemnation.*

That is why Paul emphasized in 2 Corinthians 3:6-7 that *the Law is the ministry of death; **not life.***

To live under guilt, shame and condemnation means *to be ruled by a consciousness of lack.*

In this book I want to reveal part of the secret to **appropriating truth.**

It's one thing to receive the Word of God. I mean, it's one thing to listen to the revelation of eternal truth, *but it is quite another* **to fully embrace it and allow it to impact and permeate your whole being.**

The ultimate impact of the truth is encountered and experienced only in its **appreciation;** its appropriation in your heart, *and as it **then** spills over in your life.*

But you see, too often, when we move away from the word *"**appreciation**,"* to try to study the words *"application"* or *"appropriation,"* we fall into the trap of our own effort.

I have often seen sincere Christians seeking to diligently appropriate and apply what is revealed in the Scriptures, even in the revelation of the New Testament, only to end up trapped in their own works again.

And you see, after a while they become so disappointed and discouraged in their own efforts that they go back to the old formulas prescribed for Man's efforts as defined in the Law.

So with our study in this book together I want us to receive afresh and anew, and embrace fully, the impartation and inspiration that God desires to quicken inside of us, I am talking about, the energy; the ability *that causes us to successfully appropriate what God reveals concerning us in His Word,*

…so that our appropriation may not be *a mere clumsy effort of our own,* to try and make our own, *what God has made Christ to be for us and to us,*

...yet another clumsy effort of our own, to try and make our own, **what God has already made ours** in Christ!

God wants us to discover Him, not only as the alpha of our faith, but as the Omega, as the finisher, the perfecter of our faith.

God wants us to discover ourselves in Him. He wants us to discover His initiative as the only guarantee to our success.

Hallelujah!

The only alternative to a guilt and self-achievement motivated obedience would be *a faith-inspired obedience!*

In our religious mindsets of the past we were always motivated by *'I want to give more because I am conscious of how little I've given in the past'* and *'I will begin to pray more, because I feel so self-conscious and condemned; I am conscious of the fact that I have prayed so little'* and *'I am going to begin to read the Scriptures more, because I feel self-conscious over the lack of "word" in my life: **always conscious of my lack**.'*

That kind of motivation will always cause you to be desperately disappointed.

It is absolutely imperative that we discover another kind of obedience: *a faith-motivated, faith-inspired obedience!*

While the Law limits me to my own ability to achieve, *FAITH releases me to discover His nature within me.*

Under the Law, you see, I would always feel conscious of my lack ...and thus my need for improvement in my behavior, my conduct, my attitude, and my mentality.

And so I would seek to *develop* the best part of me.

I would seek through some form of diligence and discipline to stop my hand from doing wrong, to stop my eyes from looking at the wrong thing, and to stop my mind from meditating on the wrong things.

I would seek to somehow cultivate the best of me: *only to stand condemned again and again…*

...because I remain limited and reduced to my own effort, seeing myself as, and being a fallen man!

But you see, *FAITH releases me to discover my true identity in Him; not the one of myself I have adopted, but which is a fabricated lie!*

Instead, by God's FAITH I am released to discover the nature of God that I am already a partaker of!

I am set free to discover an inexhaustible inspiration, an inexhaustible resource which dwells and abides within me!

I am set free to discover infinity; an eternal infinite realm that dwells permanently within me!

I am set free to discover the infinite One, the infinity of His person, of Himself, inspiring me and energizing me from within!

…energizing His nature,

…energizing within me His ability.

And I discover within the mirror reflection of His covenant, God's own inability to be jealous and whatever…

…God's own inability to be captive to sin.

And as I focus, through that faith awakening within my heart, upon this very gospel, upon this mirror, upon Him who is within me; upon Him who is Himself the Word who abides within me, *God Himself becomes the fuel and the energy of my life!*

Chapter 2

The Glory Of God

Would you turn with me in your own Bible to Colossians 1:25-29,

*"God entrusted me with a revelation of this mystery so that in my ministry to you I will make the word known **in its full implication**."*

When Paul says that he desires to make the word fully known, his desire is not so much for us to be such diligent students of his teaching that eventually we would be able to quote both him and the Scriptures he uses from A to Z!

When Paul says that he desires to make the word fully known, it was not so that we can have all our doctrinal definitions in line, and simply end up with a head full of theological information.

But really, when Paul says that he desires to make the word fully known, he says that his desire is to so communicate in his ministry *the full implication and the full impartation of the word* **that not one of us would lack anything of what the word declares concerning us!**

Paul desires to make the word fully known in its full implication *so that the full application of the word would be made available to our faith.*

And so, here in verse 26 he says,

*"This word contained **a hidden mystery** in past ages and generations, **but now it is <u>fully revealed</u>** to His saints!"*

*"To them God **longed to declare** the riches of the glory of this mystery **on behalf of the nations**..."*

Can you see how God **yearned** for ages **to declare *to all the nations*** what He is only now (after the coming of Christ) able to declare through His saints?

God **longed to declare fully** through the prophetic word of old *which was but a fragment of the completeness of God's purpose.*

God **yearned to reveal more** than what the prophetic word spoken through many generations could allow Him to reveal; *because it was incomprehensible in full, due to the mindsets of fallen humanity.*

He was restricted in what He could say and reveal *because of Man's hardness of heart and hardness of hearing;* Man's condition of deception and ignorance and lack of comprehension as a result of the Fall.

He yearned to reveal what He is now able to openly declare *"on behalf of all the nations."*

*"This is the mystery: **Christ in you; Christ's indwelling <u>fulfills your hope and expectation</u> for glory!"***

Listen, mankind has been designed and brought forth for applause!

When God birthed Man from within His heart, He revealed a creature that stands in the full majesty and the full glory of His own opinion!

When God invented us and designed us, He created and brought forth a being from within Himself for applause; *to enjoy His approval and His applause!*

When God brought us forth from His inner-most being, He revealed a being that He Himself as God *would not shrink from!*

When He designed us and brought us forth, He revealed a being that is in His likeness and that would <u>brightly</u> reflect His own majesty; *that would rightly reflect His own image, His own person; His very own being!*

God displays in this creature called Man, in us ...*He exhibits and displays an exact replica, an exact mirror, of His own beauty!*

So that all of heaven and all of creation could stand at attention and take note in appreciation and applause of this awesome creature ...of Man ...of us!

Romans 3:23 speaks of the fact that,

"...all have sinned and fallen short of the glory of God..."

But verse 24 says that **that same all**,

*"...they have <u>all been justified</u> freely by His grace *through the redemption that is in Jesus Christ!"*

The word *"glory"* or DOXA in the original Greek broken down to its simplest form **speaks of *an opinion; a favorable opinion.***

Do you know that Sin has robbed Man?

It has robbed us of living **in that glorious opinion of God, exhibiting the glory of His person!**

It has reduced mankind to a life defined by and restricted to mere survival in the flesh, for all intents and purposes *separated from our original design!*

It has also separated us from intimate fellowship with God, living our lives with blinders on; trapped in our isolation and inner-loneliness!

And so you see, to get back to our scripture in Colossians One, *the nations longed for, and therefore anticipated, in their hearts, in their spirits, a restoring of glory!*

There was a longing for and therefore a growing anticipation of a restoring of the correct opinion; *a restoring of the accurate definition of their lives!* Knowing all the while that every avenue they have pursued, for glory in the flesh, have failed them and left them wanting and longing for more; it has left them with the sense that; in spite of enjoying every glory the flesh can provide, *there must be more to my life than mere existence in the flesh from day to day, century to century!*

And so we see mankind, we see Man exposed and vulnerable to even more deception and hypocrisy, *through his own glory hunger.*

You see, it is because Man always hungered for someone else's positive opinion and approval, *because we were made for it!*

We were designed and made for applause; *God's ultimate approval of us, and God's ultimate applause!*

But in Man's hunger to achieve enough applause to merit his life, to justify and merit his existence, *he had no choice but became a hypocrite!*

We, mankind as a whole, progressively fell more and more *into deception and hypocrisy!*

In Ephesians 6:6, Paul says that fallen man, (everyone that has lost their way and still live ignorant of God's glory), *living their lives separated from the glory of God, separated from an intimate relationship with God,* he says that *"...**they have become men-pleasers,"*** and he makes mention of giving **mere** *"...**eye-service.**"*

"Eye-service" speaks of *trying to behave well in someone else's presence **while my real demeanor and behavior is hidden** behind*

that person's back. You see, that's what **hypocrisy** is all about.

But why would a person seek to **impress** their boss?

Why would one person seek to draw *positive approval* from another?

Because of our universal hunger of what we have lost through Adam's fall!

And so in our consciousness of lack and in our inferiority and inadequacy, we would seek to gain another standard of approval and applause *other than God's original approval and applause **already given to us from the beginning.***

And so can you now see why God had to expose the deception of our worldly standards, in terms of society's definition of wisdom, in terms of their standards, in terms of noble birth, in terms of what the world approves of?

God had to shame the who's who of society in order to rebuke their hypocrisy and awaken their hunger for the real thing *instead of the fake, inferior, make believe glory, they have been settling for!* And do you know how God did this?

He took those who were nothing, those who were despised, those who were disqualified and rejected in terms of the world's opinion, and *He elevated them, and restored their real glory to them, in the success of His Son, Jesus Christ!*

Hallelujah!

So that no flesh might boast in His presence!

So that every mouth may be stopped; *every other opinion canceled!*

So that every effort and false, fleshly self-elevation of man, even man's sincere religious self-effort, *may be condemned as a total missing of the mark in the light of the excellence of His achievement in our stead and on our behalf and to our benefit!*

He did this because of the greatness of His love and His eternal, unchanging opinion of who we truly are as His workmanship, as His design, as His offspring, as His kids, as His one of a kind masterpiece.

In that achievement, in that great act motivated by His love for us, He restored to us *everything that Adam lost* <u>*and more*</u>*!*

You see, because God brought forth a being from within Himself, in His very own likeness and image, *His redemption had to match that original image, that original likeness, that original design, that original being* **God had in mind from the very beginning!**

In Christ, in that work of redemption, *God restored fallen Man* <u>*in full*</u>*, back to His true image and to His exact likeness.*

God engineered a redemption in Christ Jesus that *fully restored us* back into God's exact image and likeness; *the fullness of it!*

We are indeed again **partakers of the Divine nature!**

And so the nations have longed for and anticipated a day that would restore to them *more than what they could achieve in the flesh, or in their religion; even in their most diligent effort.*

Let's get back to Colossians 1:27. It says how,

*"…God **longed to declare** <u>the riches of the glory of this mystery</u> on behalf of all the nations. What is the mystery: Christ is in you! That indwelling **fulfills your hope and expectation for true and lasting glory!**"*

In Haggai 2:7, Haggai speaks prophetically about Him (Christ) *being the desire of the nations.*

And so in Colossians 1:28, Paul says,

*"…we **proclaim Him** as we **awaken every man's mind and spirit,** instructing every individual, bringing them **into full enlightenment,** in order that we may **present** everyone (every single individual) **without shortcoming,** and fully efficient in Christ"*

So, when Paul says that,

"…my desire and the urgency of my ministry is to make the Word (the message, the gospel)

fully *known,* **in its full implication,**" it is not just so that he could get it off his chest, and fulfill some obligation, by following some kind of formula that he knows he's got to preach ...or else.

No, he sees and anticipates the end product in every individual as he clearly sees every man, every person, every single individual **already complete** *and now also* **mature** *in Christ.*

He presents them before his Father as a trophy of his Father's grace, as a trophy of Jesus' triumph: **blameless, innocent, without reproach, as the end-product of God's design and God's redemptive plan** *set forth through His Son, Jesus.*

And so Paul does not shrink back from this gospel of grace. He does not feel *embarrassed* about what he has to say, neither does he feel *intimidated* and *inferior,* or *a failure,* when, along life's road, he encounters someone disapproving of his message, or when he encounters someone disappointing him; even if it is one of his own disciples, like Demas perhaps, forsaking him.

His own personal confidence in the truth revealed in Christ cannot be shaken, neither can his confidence in boldly proclaiming that good news, that truth, in his message!

He doesn't even feel intimidated when he encounters some misconduct **that is not in line with the life expression of** <u>a believer</u>

redeemed to be the reflection, the very mirror of Him, who is our life: Jesus.

Listen, there is a knowledge in Paul's spirit **that is stronger** *than any contradiction to his confidence and to his message.*

You see, Paul has a knowledge and **persuasion** *that propels an energy and an inspiration within him* **to continue to present** *every man, every person, every individual* – even the weakest, lowliest, rejected one: the nobody – *as a mirror reflection of God's own majesty; of the majesty of **His very being,** without apology.*

Why?

Because He Himself, Jesus, is not ashamed to be associated with you and to call you His brother! - Hebrews 2:11.

He is not ashamed of the human race; *He is not embarrassed to associate with us!* **Because He knows who we truly are!**

...Despite the false expressions of the inferior identities we have embraced as our true identity, *based on the lies and deception we have believed and embraced about ourselves, and lived!*

Hey, your conduct *cannot define you; not even your failure can!*

Even while you were yet hostile in your mind and evil deeds, *it did not keep Him* *from loving you with an eternal, immovable, steadfast love!*

It did not hinder or restrain Him from giving His all to you!

It did not even remotely dampen His effort in winning you back to His heart!

Isn't it wonderful to consider the awesomeness of His love for you?!

...of His affection towards us all?!

Isn't it simply mind-blowing and magnificent to meditate **upon His initiative?!**

One of my friends said the other day on Facebook, and it's true, that *the more you meditate upon the initiative of God,* **the more immune you become to condemnation.**

Ha... ha... ha...

God's initiative in His love **seals your immunity to inferiority!**

When you discover the initiative of God that He undertook in His love, *to rescue our minds out of ignorance, to win back our affections* while we were yet hostile towards Him – while *I* was yet hostile towards Him – **it totally wins my heart!**

How much more now that I am reconciled shall I be saved from my fear of wrath and from all sorts of condemnation as well as my sense of inferiority!

Hallelujah!

Thank you Father for your steadfast love!

Father today, even here, in the here and now, we want to honor You.

We want to honor You for Your prevailing heart towards us.

We want to honor You for Your prevailing favor, Father, upon our lives.

We simply are in awe of You!

We are in awe in Your most immediate, most intimate presence, oh God.

We worship You as the Alpha and the Omega, the One who began a good work within us, by Your Spirit, through Your Word!

Yes, we worship You, Alpha and Omega, the One who is able to so perfect that understanding and working which You have authored within us, *to such a degree **that we too would stand and be in the same glory, in the same majesty** wherein Your Son, Jesus, was revealed in the flesh.*

And Father, today, in Your Gospel, in this book even, we behold His glory, the glory of the One begotten only of the Father and not of the will of the flesh, not of some lie, some false fallen expression.

Father, we behold His glory, *full of grace **and truth.***

Thank you Father. How we honor You in our hearts today! How we honor Your Son, Jesus! How we honor your work, *as we simply reflect on and then reflect your workmanship!*

Thank you Lord.

Thank you, my Father.

Hallelujah!

And so Paul says in Colossians 1:28,

*"...**we proclaim Him, as we awaken every man's mind and spirit.**"*

Would you also take a look with me at Colossians 1:5.

Well, let's start from Colossians 1:3.

Chapter 3

Holy Spirit Imparted Revelation Knowledge

Paul writes this letter of Colossians to a few believers who lived, just a few miles up the road, past Laodicea, in a small mountain town, called: Colossi, along the old "Spice" trading route, later known as the "Silk Road" going north, to China, from Ephesus. Colossi is a town that today no longer exists.

Paul's letter was addressed to a group of believers that he had yet to meet in the flesh. He only heard the testimony of their faith through Epaphras, one of his disciples who went to Laodicea and Colossi and ministered the gospel to these people.

Their testimony so inspired Paul because it immediately attached their faith to his own, independent of any kind of formal or informal registration or of any kind of label that some denomination could limit them to.

No, there was something much stronger between them and Paul. There was an inner witness burning in both Paul's heart and theirs that tied them together, which they *embraced together in the same New Covenant realities.*

And so it was this inner witness and love with which his heart was awakened for them that inspired him to write this letter after he listened to Epaphras' testimony about their response to, *about their embrace of*, the gospel.

And so Paul says there in Colossians 1:3-5,

"Every time I pray for you, I thank God for you."

"I have heard the testimony of your faith in Christ Jesus, and the love which you have towards all the saints,"

"…knowing that **you have discovered the absolute fulfillment** *of your hope and dream* **in everything that was laid up for you** *in heavenly places (the unseen realm of spirit-realities). This all (the discovery of these things and the sense of fullness and fulfillment it brought you)* **<u>this</u> was first awakened in you <u>when the truth</u> of the gospel dawned on you***."*

You see, Paul realized that the anticipation of the nations, the hope of the nations *to again be restored to a glory that they had lost,* which they knew they were no longer enjoying within them, *would be resurrected and quickened and awakened and stirred up through the gospel.*

He says in Verse 6,

"The same impact the word of the gospel has had in your lives is also experienced everywhere else in the world where this gospel is preached. And so the day you heard and understood the grace of God (the revelation of

44

God's absolute favor upon you, because of His immense love for you) the gospel began to bear fruit and increase among you..."

"...just as you were taught and discipled by Epahpras, our precious fellow servant, who is a faithful minister of Christ on our behalf; he is the very extension of our ministry to you."

And then Paul continues to just elaborate on his confidence in their faith experience.

Also in the next chapter he says how he has experienced in his own heart a knitting together with them in God, by the Spirit, through the same word, the same gospel, the same faith, *through their common instruction, their common revelation that they all now enjoy together.*

What we all enjoy together in the gospel is so beautiful, but I want us to get back to Colossians 1:28.

Paul says,

*"**Him** we proclaim **as we awaken every person's mind and spirit,** every individual's mind and spirit, instructing every single individual, bringing them **into full enlightenment,** in order that we may **present** them **complete** and **absolutely without shortcoming,** fully efficient in Christ."*

Remember now our theme in this book; we are studying **faith inspired obedience.**

And we are studying this **faith inspired obedience** *in the light of our appropriation of the truth of what the gospel reveals.*

Precisely so that our efforts in appropriating what God reveals in the gospel will no longer limit us to ourselves, to our own willpower and struggles, *but **that Holy Spirit imparted revelation, our insight and comprehension into the truth of the gospel, which comes from Him alone, will release us to a faith inspired obedience, to a faith-action, a faith-working within us, through our appreciation of that truth revealed, which will bring us into a place in our hearts of fully inheriting and possessing the complete wealth of everything that is ours in Him.***

And so, there in the next verse, Colossians 1:29, Paul writes, and he says,

"This, then, is the focus of my labor and intense involvement with you."

Do you see that in Paul's ministry there is no hint of casual, mere superficial involvement?

There is no hint of just casually, even half-heartedly, just so-so performing the work of the ministry. *'Because, you see, it's my lot and my destiny in life to be a pastor, even though I didn't really even want to do it, but God called me to this, and so I have to just keep preaching and survive on my own teaching, and through my preaching abilities, living on barely get along street, next to grumble ally.'*

46

No man, if that's your attitude and your level of revelation you might as well quit the ministry. You are not doing Jesus any favors!

Actually you are doing more harm than good!

Listen, there is a certain kind of diligent excellence, a specific attractive life-energy, a joy, a love, and a passion that is alive in Paul's heart and *which is inspired within him, **in his focus; in what he sees so clearly.***

Where does it come from?

From a sense of duty and guilt?

From a sense of, *'well, you know, if I don't preach enough, then maybe people won't give me enough money, and if I don't preach enough then God won't be pleased with me anymore either. If I am not diligent enough and get up early enough, at the earliest hour of the morning, and if I don't have such a full schedule and such a full program to such a degree that everyone else is impressed with me, then people are going to lose their esteem of me, and worse yet, I am going to lose God's favor upon my life and ministry.'* No man, nonsense!

Where does Paul get his energy resource from to minister with such life, such anointing, such inspiration, such joy, such love, and such attractive excellence?

Paul says that *"it is according to the inspiration of God's energy that He so powerfully works within me..."*

Another translation says *"it is by His active energy which is mightily working in me..."*

Notice what the Amplified version says. It says,

"...striving with all the super human energy which He so mightily kindles and works within me..."

In Paul's own experience of that super human energy, *he is at the same time quickening and kindling that same energy in his disciples' hearts.*

He is duplicating his own experience of God's intense love; he is duplicating his own experience *of **a power resource** in that love, that is larger than what human toil and effort could ever experience.*

It is bigger than what any exploit, or any act of my own effort, could ever draw from.

And so you see, Paul's total desire for us is to tap into that same secret, **into that same revelation and understanding of the truth of the gospel; *into the love of God, and the faith of God,*** *and therefore also into that same enjoyment and spontaneous energy that is mightily kindled within us.*

All this is nothing other than God's Spirit-working by which He works inside of us!

By the accurate revelation of the truth of the gospel; *of the love of God and of the*

faith of God, God is at work within us both to will and to do of His good pleasure!

And all this is our portion, **holding fast the word of life;** *simply focusing upon, and indulging in and enjoying, what we see, in the truth of the gospel!*

Hallelujah!

And you see, these things are not complicated; **the love of God is not complicated,** *even the babes can enjoy it,* and thus experience *for themselves, the power of God at work within them!*

Chapter 4

Knitted Together Through Faith

In Colossians 2:1 Paul says,

*"I want you to know **the intensity** of my labor on your behalf and on behalf of those believers in Laodicea and all those who have not yet seen me face to face in the flesh."*

*"My **desire for you** is to be **greatly encouraged** in your hearts as we are all being **knitted together** or, **welded together**…"*

That same Greek word, **sunbibazo** that is being used there for *"knitted together" or "welded together"* is the same word used in 1 Corinthians 2:16 for *"**instructed together**,"* where it says,

"Who has known the mind of the Lord so as to instruct Him?"

So, 1 Corinthians 2:16 would be much better translated as to say, *"Who has known the mind of the Lord, **so as to be "knitted together" with Him, or to be "welded together" with Him?"***

*"**But we have the mind of Christ!**"*

*"…therefore we do have the mind of the Lord and can be "**knitted together**" or "**welded**"*

*together" with Him, or **made one with Him,*** *through being "instructed together" by **the*** ***truth** revealed in the gospel!"*

I added that last bit in there, but Paul could have just as easily said it as well, ha... ha... ha...

Paul communicates this same thought, this same concept again, when he uses that exact same Greek word **sunbibazo** in Ephesians 4:16 when he says,

"Out of Him (Christ Jesus), *every joint in the body is **fitted together, (literally)** <u>through words</u>.)*

Ephesians 2:21 says, *"In Him the whole building* (the whole body of believers, the whole temple of God, the whole New Jerusalem, the whole Zion, speaking of the whole body of believers in Christ Jesus) *perfectly **fits together** and arises into a sanctuary (a permanent dwelling place and abode) of the Lord."*

(Note: The Greek word, **sunarmologoumenon** used here is a combination of four Greek words: **sun** – together, **armos** – joint, **logos** – word, **meno** – to abide. Thus, *"**joined together, through the abiding word**."*)

Ephesians 4:16 says,

"Out of Him (Christ Jesus), *every joint in the body is **fitted together, <u>through words</u>,** and every ligament is **knitted together** (or **<u>instructed</u> together** – **sunbibazo**, as in 1*

52

Corinthians 2:16 and also then there in Colossians 2:2)

*"...every joint in the body is **fitted together, through words,** and every ligament is **knitted together,** as every individual part **contributes** its measure (enjoying **the same** confession or conversation)."*

*"**This is <u>the exact same energy</u> that makes spontaneous growth possible, and combustible, in <u>love</u>***" (It is all in there, it's all wrapped up in God's revealed love plan)*

*"...**<u>love</u> being the environment that sustains this growth and this passion (it's the very focus of our confession, of our whole conversation with God, and with one another).***"*

(Note 1 Corinthians 2:13. *It is* **words:** the **truth** of the gospel **revealed** and **made known** in other words, *it is that* **word** concerning the eternal Word, concerning the eternal LOGAO (the eternal **conversation**) made flesh, ***which combine*** *spirit with spirit* – **<u>words</u> combine Spirit with spirit. (Discovering *that eternal conversation made flesh* combines Spirit with spirit).**)

God's conversation, God's revealed love plan, *which is the source of all this,* is **made known** in Ephesians 3:17-19. Paul says that,

*"...you will become thoroughly rooted and firmly established in the love plan of God, **<u>drawing</u> your nourishment from His love***

revealed; from His love revelation of Himself, in Christ Jesus. I am talking about discovering that revelation concerning His love for you, and then finding your strength and stability in that love revealed."

"Faith brings the **consciousness** *of Christ's permanent* **residence (of His permanency, and of His love, and of the permanency of that love)** *into your heart."*

(Or: *"This is the urgency of my desire, that* **your capacity to accommodate the indwelling Christ will be greatly enlarged** *through the working of His power, through the working of His truth and of His love, in your inner man."*

"The wealth of His glory (of His favorable opinion) measures this power; it measures His ability at work within you.*")*

Verse 18 & 19,

"Then you will take **full possession,** *together with all the saints, of* **the limitless dimension of His love.** *You will* **thoroughly comprehend** *the breadth and the length and the height and the depth, and* **intimately, fully know,** *the love of Christ which* **exceeds** *every limit of sense-governed knowledge.* **It is within the scope of this unveiling of reality, and it becoming reality to you, that the fullness of God will flood your life!"**

Paul goes on to say in verse 20 that,

"God's superabundant ability to do something by His love within our hearts is the exact power that now energizes us from within."

Verse 21 says,

*"His glory is therefore now manifested **within** and **through** the church…"*

(The Greek word for "church" is: EKKLESIA, meaning that God's glory is now manifested within **those who see their true identity as revealed in their origin,** and so they are thereby **called out of darkness,** out of the fallen mentality of the world; out of the HADES, out of that **hell,** out of that **spiritual blindness,** *into His marvelous light!*)

*"His glory is now manifested therefore, both **in the church** …and in Christ Jesus, **as an eternal trophy, throughout all generations.** Amen."*

Hallelujah!

In other words, what God is now able to manifest through us, His church *(through those who see their true origin and identity in Him)* **is not in any way inferior to what He was able to communicate of Himself in Christ Jesus!**

You see it is exactly this **being knitted together with Him,** being **welded together** with Him, **in His love,** *that is the very secret to God's energy released in your spirit.*

It is the very secret of His release in your mind, of you drawing from His power, of your tapping into the revelation and the excellence and the power of His word, (not merely through a natural diligence that keeps you limited to a mere meditation of the law without revelation,) *but a new diligence is awakened within you which sets you free.*

Discover His love for you fully; *discover that wellspring of life,* **discover the artesian well of His ability and His energy at work within you, amen.**

But let's get back to Colossians 2 there.

Paul says there in verse 2,

*"My desire for you is to be encouraged in your hearts, as we are all being **knitted together** or **welded together**…"*

The rest of verse 2 says,

*"…**united in all the richness of being** <u>**fully persuaded**</u> **(of His love for us and for all others)** <u>**through insight.**</u>"*

You see, when I make the word **known** in its **full implication** *there is a supernatural enlightenment that comes to your understanding.*

And that **insight** that is birthed within your spirit **knits you to the mind of God.**

It knits you to the heart of God; to more than mere head-knowledge and religious doctrine.

It knits you to more than just another philosophical definition of some biblical truth, more than just another philosophical definition *about God.*

It knits you to the mind of God as <u>the very expression</u> of the heart of God.

It literally knits you to the ever living God Himself; *to the very heart of your one and only true Father.*

And you see, through that literal, practical, real knitting together with Him, *God's energy begins to well up within you!*

Hallelujah!

*"...**united with Him, in all the richness of being <u>fully persuaded</u> through insight, <u>intelligently grasping the love of God</u>; the hidden purpose of God in Christ."***

Through the ages religion has watered down this baptism (this **immersion**) to something so far inferior to what we are talking about. They have watered it down to the practice of rituals, the practice of water baptism: *a mere act of obedience in the flesh, a mere outward sign or symbol.* They have watered down **our immersion into Him who is love** as to the mere act of getting wet and getting dry.

But you see it is so wonderful to come to a new understanding, and to encounter, through the full embrace of the truth of His gospel, ***that true immersion*** into the Father, and into Christ

Jesus, and into the Spirit of God Himself, and into His love, and into the body of Christ!

There truly is only one baptism, one *immersion* of any real consequence!

It is our full immersion into faith; *into the very faith of God, into the mind and heart of the Father, into His love,* exactly as it was displayed in our Lord Jesus Christ, and then revealed to us by the Holy Spirit, through the apostles, and especially apostle Paul.

Paul confirmed this when he made it plain in 1 Corinthians 1:17,

*"For Christ did not send me to baptize (in water), **but to preach the gospel"***

I am not against the practice of water baptism as an outward sign of an inward change, or even as a mere act of obedience, yielding to the Lordship of Jesus and to the Spirit of Christ speaking through the New Testament Scriptures. **But understanding, with insight, God's purpose in the death of His Son, wherewith He has united us to Himself; *that understanding,* that revelation, *that insight,* that appropriation, that embrace, that full immersion into the love of God, into God Himself, that full immersion which takes place within us, within our hearts, *is of the utmost importance.***

I say again: **It's the only immersion of any real consequence!**

Our full appropriation, our full embrace, our correct understanding, our revelation and accurate insight into that death and resurrection – which water baptism is only a picture of – *is all that really matters,* **according to Paul.**

Hallelujah!

Paul continues and he says there in Colossians 2:3,

"The wealth of wisdom and knowledge concealed in the life of Christ (**and through the gospel now revealed**) *is our treasure."*

Chapter 5

Confess His Provision, Not Your Problem

And now Verse 5 of Colossians 2 says,

"Even though I am physically absent from you, yet I am one with you in spirit. I am delighted to witness the consistency and strength of your faith in Christ."

He says,

"I am delighted to witness the consistency and strength of your faith…"

I want you to notice that he is not referring to the consistency of behavior, of good moral conduct, but to **the consistency and strength of their faith!**

Why?

Look at verse 6,

(Let me just throw out this question while I am on this subject: Does consistency of faith excuse inconsistency of behavior? By no means!)

But let's continue to study from the Scriptures,

Now our regular translations say, Colossians 2:6,

"Just as you have received Christ, so walk in Him."

But listen to this translation of that scripture, and don't worry: it's the same; it is just a little more expounding… ha… ha… ha…

"Just as you have embraced Christ Jesus the Lord…"

How did you do it?

Through the hearing of faith, amen!

"Just as you have been introduced…"

"Just as you have received…"

"Just as you have embraced the beginning of His working within you…"

How did you receive the beginning of His working within you?

How did you receive the beginning of God's involvement within you, of God's working within your heart, within your inner-man?

It started happening when when you heard the truth of the gospel and faith came alive in you!

…and "faith worketh by love," amen.

It was through the hearing of the truth of the gospel. It was through the hearing of the truth of His love for you! It was through the hearing of faith; God's Faith!

It was through hearing *with faith,* amen.

You were not immersed into fellowship and relationship with Father God, and with Jesus Christ, and with the Holy Spirit *because you confessed your sins in detail.*

There is absolutely no reference in the New Testament that links the confession of sin to the new birth!

The only place where John speaks of it is in 1 John Chapter One. He says in Verse Nine that the one walking in deception and still thinking that he is in fellowship *must* **confess** (**HOMOLOGAO** in the Greek; HOMO, **the same,** LOGAO, **conversation,** thus, he must **develop the same conversation God has** about) *his sin.*

And John was writing that to the *"little children."*

Paul speaks of this subject in another place and says that, *"...when it comes to evil, **I would have you be innocent concerning it, just as little children,** but when it comes to <u>understanding</u> I would have you be mature!"*

You will notice in that same chapter of 1 John, that John also refers to *"the youth, the young men,"* **who have already overcome the evil one.** Then he also refers to *"the fathers."*

Thus he is referring to the different stages of maturity in understanding; in mentality and thinking and in strength of spirit and in experience. *It comes though revelation and insight and understanding into the truth of the successful work of redemption.*

1 John 1:9 has been preached for years as a very convenient excuse for sin.

While he is writing to the *"little children,"* the immature ones, still stumbling in their understanding and thus in their walk, he says in 1 John 2:1-2, *"**I am writing this** to you,"* in other words *"I am bringing more revelation and understanding to you, deeper insight, **so that you may not sin**."*

*"...but if anyone does sin, if anyone does have an accident, if anyone does trip up and falls, **we have an advocate**..."*

Actually the word is PERACLETOS, and not advocate, as so many of our translations has it, PARACLETOS meaning, *"**One who comforts us with the truth, the truth about our true identity as children of God; not children of the father of lies, meaning, the Devil. And He defends our innocence with the truth of what he accomplished for us in the successful work of redemption, and thus He upholds our freedom: Jesus Christ!**"*

That is my own paraphrased version, but all I am saying in all of this is that *confession of sin,* in terms of you telling the detail of your sin and your past to God **has no value, no merit,** *as far as your redemption is concerned.*

The Bible teaches and makes it clear all over the New Testament that it is through your hearing with faith, that something wells up within you!

It is a conviction in your heart!

A belief and a total persuasion that believes that God raised Jesus from the dead, *because your sins were removed from you as far as the east is from the west!*

That's what wells up in your heart. It's a whole new, brand new **conversation** we enter into, within ourselves, within our hearts!

That's what hearing with faith tells us.

It tells you that *when your sins were absolutely forgiven you and cast into the sea of forgetfulness it is then when God raised Jesus from the dead because of your justification.*

It all happened on your behalf for your justification, *and then He was raised because of your justification* according to Romans 4:25.

So instead of you still getting all entangled in a confession of sin, *you instead know and discover afresh for yourself what your faith confesses?* It doesn't confess your sin; it starts a whole new conversation about your sin; *it confesses Jesus Christ as your Savior.*

Faith's confession, faith's conversation is not sin!

Faith's confession, faith's conversation is Jesus Christ!

Faith's confession and conversation is a **successful** redemption **accomplished** in Him!

I say again: Faith's confession, faith's conversation, is not sin, in all its ugliness!

You see, it is that faith conversation within yourself, with yourself; ***it is the very faith conversation and consequent confession of Him as your provision*** *that releases you!*

You can continue to confess your sickness if you want, and tell God the very detail of your sickness, *and you will not get better.*

But when you start perceiving and understanding and embracing God's conversation with you in Christ; that word of truth, concerning your healing in Him, by His stripes, ***then a faith will be quickened in your heart that will begin to come in agreement with the truth you have embraced.***

You will start to have a new confession and will begin to confess Jesus and His work of redemption as Savior and Lord, reigning supreme over every contradiction that might still want to plague your heart, your mind, your spirit, and your body.

I am telling you that in discovering the accurate revelation and insight and full understanding of God's work of redemption, a faith will be quickened within you that will begin to confess

Jesus as your Lord, as your Savior, and your Healer! A faith will be quickened within you that will begin to confess Him as God's provision on your behalf, *and that faith will begin to lay a hold of the healing that is yours already.*

So, if you want to tap into the secret of His working within you, you need to parallel that to the initial contact that you had with God, when the gospel first dawned on you; *when faith was first awakened within you, through understanding the truth of the gospel; grasping the love God has for you!*

You see, you may not have had it all together. You may not have understood all mysteries, but you grasped something, you understood something: **the love of God for you,** and something called faith came alive in you. ***You knew and understood the love God has for you*** *and in that understanding, in the hearing of faith, in that hearing with faith,* ***there was an encounter that took place*** *between you and God that was* ***very real*** *and it changed your thinking and your life; it set you on a whole new path!*

As long as that love is held onto, as long as that faith is kept alive, *that encounter continues and that relationship and fellowship, that ongoing faith conversation, is kept vibrant and alive.*

When your heart first responded to Him in love and He embraced you through the hearing of faith, and you embraced Him back through the hearing with faith, *that hearing with faith released the energy of God, the redemption power of God* that literally snatched you away from the clutches of darkness, ignorance, and confusion, and restored you to God.

That very hearing with faith released redemptive power, the very energy of God within your inner-man. It translated you out of the kingdom of the evil one and literally brought you into the kingdom of His Son and of His life. It restored you to God Himself!

That hearing with faith canceled that document, *in your mind,* which stood against you with its legal demands, and its condemnation, and shame, and guilt and inferiority.

The power of God on display in your life, on display in your inner-man as the "alpha", as the beginning, as the initiator of all this, it came into your life as *a direct result of the truth of the gospel dawning upon your understanding and upon your heart.* It came as a direct result of the hearing with faith!

And so Paul says in Colossians 2:6,

"Just as you have received and embraced Christ…"

How did you receive Christ?

How did you embrace Christ?

Through your own works?

Through your own diligent confession and repentance, and feelings of regret and remorse?

Through your own crying and begging and sobbing?

No man.

My book on *"Confession of sin & Freedom from it"* as well as my Study Course called, *"The Gospel In 3-D!"* delves deeper into this subject and these things and will help you understand it better.

Listen, the good news is not revealing to Man the poverty of his condition *but the wealth of God's provision, already given to him, in Jesus Christ!*

Good news is not revealing to Man the poverty of his condition. That's not good news, brethren!

If I told the poor man, *"Behold how poor you are,"* there is no good news in that.

But let me tell you, **the Good News is all about revealing the wealth of God's provision in Christ Jesus** *in spite of Man's poverty stricken state, in spite of a person's spiritually poor condition!*

Hallelujah!

Chapter 6

Standing Complete in Faith

So Paul says,

"Just as you have received and embraced Christ Jesus…"

Through the hearing of faith, and through hearing with faith, amen.

*"Just as you have received and embraced Christ Jesus, **so walk in Him.**"*

*"…**just so**"*

Through the hearing of faith, and through hearing with faith, amen!

Another translation actually says,

*"Just as you have received Christ Jesus, **through hearing with faith**…"*

That word *"received,"* is the Greek word DEGOMAI and it literally means, **to embrace.**

*"Just as you have embraced Christ Jesus, **through hearing with faith, so (or just so) conduct your whole life in the consciousness of your union with Him.**"*

"So conduct your whole life," not in the consciousness of how I lack in my own

character, in my own personality, and maybe I also need to become thirty years old like Jesus, or grow and mature more, maybe for thirty more years, *until I finally escape out of my old self and finally break free from that thing, before He can entrust me with the ministry of His word...*

...As if there is any merit in being a sinner for thirty years, *before I finally **fully embrace** and **believe** the gospel and begin to **live** as an **actual** child of God...*

Just last month I was talking to some guy about certain problems commonly faced in many other ministries and as a matter of fact also in his ministry, and I was trying to help him. But he proceeded to try and tell me that he can see how a mature saint can be a responsible witness to this word we preach about our identity already restored to us fully in Christ Jesus, but he just couldn't accept the fact that these young people we bring into our home and into the ministry can maturely walk in these things.

He basically said: *'I cannot accept the fact that these young people can be responsible enough to bear witness to the truth of the gospel, these young people you are bringing into your church and releasing into the ministry. They are simply not old enough yet, we must leave them to the world and let them party until they've had enough and then maybe they will be tempered enough through facing life's circumstances and consequences, and* the world would have matured them enough to be of any real use in the ministry.'

And so when I confronted him about the stupidity of that statement, he said: *'Brother, I don't want to pick a fight, but all I am saying is that maybe we need to let them remain sinners until they are about thirty years old so that at least they can gain some real life-experience in the world.'*

With a mindset like that, no wonder this guy's church and many others like it are in trouble.

What a ridiculous fantasy he lives in when Paul himself, referring to his own experience in the world and also in a religion very similar to this guy's says, *"whatever gain I had, I count it as refuse!"*

Paul says, *"There is absolutely no comparison. Anything and everything that experience taught me, there is nothing in it, no gain whatsoever, nothing worth hanging on to, there is **no comparison to the excellence of the knowledge of Jesus, to the wealth that I have received through the instruction in His excellence**."*

"Because you see, experience only taught me to be a hypocrite. It only taught me to be puffed up in pride, it only taught me the art of self-righteousness, it taught me how to justify myself before others, even lying to myself and to others. It taught me to rely on my own works and my own efforts to win the approval of others, to please myself and others through

my own conduct, so that I could soothe my own conscience with it. Experience only taught me how to fool myself and others, and how to appear to stand blameless in my own conduct; to strive and to be the best little Paul (...or is it Saul) I can be…"

He says, ***"But His grace taught me something better. His grace taught me that I am the product of His love, of His design and of His very own perfection, and of His in depth investment in my heart!"***

Hallelujah!

And now he says,

*"Just as you have embraced Christ, through hearing with faith, **just so**…"*

"…that same secret is yours in your application of His life in and through you."

*"…walking conscious, not of weakness, not of lack within myself, that I now have to cover up and try and bolster within myself through deception, convinced of the lie that, 'Oh, I am so young that now I have to live and struggle many more years, before I can get anywhere,' no, **but conscious of my union with Him!"***

"Listen that's your treasure!"

That's your treasure, amen, *your union with Christ* ...His treasure, His wealth, *yours!* His wisdom, *yours!* His righteousness, *your portion already!* His redemption, *fully yours!*

And so now **who I am is the very product of His word and of His truth at work within me! I am not the product of my own development of my person over time! His word of truth is what develops the maturity of Christ and its full expression in me and in my life!**

By the grace of God I am what I am!

I want to state this very emphatically here in black in white, that if the enemy of our faith could snare you with just a little leaven of your own works, of your own diligence, and your own supposed character development, then he will successfully wedge again, in-between you and God, *a consciousness of lack and inferiority.*

And then he tells you that the only way to get yourself out of that, is to be motivated by that, *to improve.*

And you know what it creates?

Even more *condemnation!* An even greater consciousness *of lack and inferiority!*

Just exactly what does the law inspire?

Works, striving, toil, frustration, exhaustion, distance, separation, and death!

It is the word PANEROS in the Greek, *the very definition of the word: evil.*

It refers to my own efforts and works, to my own labor, toil, and striving in the flesh, *to*

improve on who I already am, which produces nothing but frustration, exhaustion, and a sense of distance, and separation! *It only produces death!*

Hey listen, If works can get you **any closer to God** then works would be fine, but it can't: *it actually produces the exact opposite of closeness, and of a sense of union, and oneness with God.*

Let me just quickly read Colossians 2:7 before we move on to the next scripture.

Verse 7 says,

"What you have been taught in Him, (in Christ) **is now increasingly confirmed in your life.***"*

Remember now, *"Just as I have received Christ, I am walking* **conscious of my union with Him,** *conscious of* **what I have been taught** *…"*

…the gospel of Jesus Christ, **the truth** of the **successful** work of redemption, **accomplished** in Him, is what I have been **accurately** taught,

…and that grace revelation, *revealed God's favor,* and it dawned upon my heart, and awakened me in my spirit to **righteousness.**

"…so what I have been taught <u>is now increasingly confirmed in my life</u>, **as I continue to draw nourishment from Him,***"*

*"…**being rooted in Him**,"* says Paul,

76

*"…**your gratitude** will be **the abundant evidence** of His **life, and joy, and peace, and faith, and maturity, and power,** in you!"*

It is so difficult to stop here, because there is so much more that Paul has to say to us in this book of Colossians, and you are welcome to go read and study it further on your own, and perhaps I will cover it again in some of my future books, I do highly recommend reading and studying it in the Mirror Study Bible as well, so much are made so abundantly clear there, but I want us to move on from Colossians and quickly go and have a look at the weakness of the Law.

Chapter 7

The Weakness Of The Law

A focus upon the Law is a focus upon myself and it keeps me limited to my own effort to change my behavior and change my conduct.

In Matthew 5, Jesus refers to the Law and do you know what He says?

He basically says that faith in the gospel leaves you without excuse to be less diligent than what you would have been under the Law.

Faith does not mean that there is now a relaxing of the life the Law portrays.

Jesus said that if you relax even one of the least of the commandments you might as well relax the whole thing and admit your hypocrisy because you break the whole thing and make it of no consequence: *you make it of no effect!*

Don't interpret faith and grace as a weak excuse to now implement a lower-standard law or *to now live a lesser life!*

Listen, no matter what you think of the Law, *it was done away with in Christ and therefore is no longer something to live by in the life of a New Testament saint, because the Law was and is a mere expression of God's desire and design for*

the quality of life He anticipated for you from the beginning, and anticipates for you still!

But what I want us to see is that, **while under the Law,** *whether the Law of Moses, Islamic Law, society's laws, or whatever other moral conscience law or code of conduct we try to live by,* **while under that Law,** outside of a proper insight and understanding of the gospel, **under the law,** not the gospel, not under grace but under the law, *while under the law,* **my own effort becomes reduced to that of** *a fallen creature.*

Remember, the demand of the Law was upon a person who was fallen **in their mind and spirit; in their mentality,** *and therefore in their nature, or conduct.*

But you see, as I now discover the perfect Law: the law of faith, the law of liberty, the law of life in Christ Jesus, **I suddenly also discover that I am actually tapping into a nature which is of God, a nature which is equal to His own,** a nature that does not just try and blindly do what the Law requires, as a requirement, dogmatically, under obligation, *but to excel in, **naturally expressing the very life** of the Law; **the very life** the Law is supposed to be all about, **but is only a shadow of!***

Hallelujah! Do you see that with me?

I am trying to introduce an accurate understanding of grace and of the truth of the gospel here, *not make excuses for sin.*

…So *please, don't quote me as preaching an excuse for sin.* That is the furthest thing from my mind.

I do understand that many of these thoughts and concepts are new to those who have grown up with a watered down, inaccurate version of the gospel.

They often get confused easily by what we teach, not because we teach confusion, *but because they are trying to marry their doctrine with ours and it doesn't work.*

I often giggle at first when I hear their cries for balance and then I grieve for them and pray for them within my spirit, because it only reveals their ignorance and their desperate need for a greater, more accurate revelation of grace than what they currently possess.

You cannot balance grace with the law and neither can you balance faith with unbelief.

There is no such thing as hyper-grace or too much righteousness teaching.

An accurate understanding of righteousness, and the work of redemption, of the gospel of grace and righteousness *is the very balance that balances and sorts out all our doctrines and corrects them all and brings them into accuracy.*

The accurate understanding of that righteousness which is revealed in the gospel *brings all things into subjection to the knowledge of Him,* and thoroughly

deals with sin, *without even focusing on sin.*

You can always get a few more of my books with titles like: *No Longer Looking for Applause, God's Measure Verses Man's Measure, Resurrection Life Now, Reigning in Righteousness* and many others if you want to understand this concept of righteousness a little better.

Please turn with me to Acts 13:38-39.

"Let it be known to you brethren that through this man (referring to Jesus Christ) *forgiveness of sins are proclaimed to you."*

On what basis is forgiveness of sins proclaimed?

Luke says,

*"...and by Him, **everyone that believes** is freed from everything from which you could not be freed by the Law of Moses."*

Why could you not be freed by the Law of Moses?

I mean why was the Law of Moses inadequate in its ability to release me rather than condemn me?

The Law was inadequate to release the human race, because it dealt with fallen Man *in his fallen mindset, in his ignorance, confusion, and deception **during a time of broken relationship.***

To release the human race was not its purpose. It had a twofold purpose, but its purpose was never to release Man and set Man free.

The double purpose of the Law was *to show Man the weakness of our own effort,* especially if measured by the standard of the Law, and secondly *to awaken in Man a longing to again stand innocent before God,* a longing after the life the Law points to, *a longing after that kind of a quality life lived in fellowship and friendship and oneness with God.*

The Law was designed to awaken within you **a frustration in your own phony hypocritical effort,** *but at the same time **it also awakens a hunger to stand innocent before God.***

The Law leads to the need for and hopefully eventual embrace of faith.

Its conclusion leaves Man frustrated and searching, looking again for something else, something greater, *and thus it inevitably leads you to an embrace of Jesus Christ and an awakening of faith.* It leads you to a discovery of the real answer, a discovery of **the truth** <u>**as it is revealed in Christ**</u>. He is the **true** way. He introduces **the very fulfillment** *of the life* merely pointed to in the Law.

Thus, the frustration and promise of the Law is meant to lead Man to the awakening of faith.

Let's quickly look at Romans 8:1-3.

"There is therefore now no condemnation to those who are in Christ Jesus..."

Does that mean that there is some condemnation towards some people who still do not know that they are in Christ Jesus?

1 Corinthians 1:30 says,

"Of God are you in Christ..."

What Paul wrote here in Romans 8:1 and 1 Corinthians 1:30 is inspired by a revelation that

"One died for all, therefore all have died!" – 2 Corinthians 5:14

In 2 Corinthians 5:19 Paul continues to expound on the implications of that revelation and He says that,

"God no longer counts our trespasses against us!"

So does God still count the world's trespasses against them?

If He does, *then there is no gospel,* no good news to proclaim to the world,

...and then we're back to good news which only apply to us who have properly responded somewhere along the line, to try and please God, by jumping through the right hoops to obey God's Law; God's command to REPENT *...or else!*

Hey, that's a different gospel my friends, that's the wrong gospel; that's no good news at all –

it's an inferior message; it's nothing but a legalistic message, *another form of the Law of Moses!*

Listen, the gospel, the good news to be made known to the entire world is founded upon the fact that *there is* **THEREFORE now no condemnation!** *(Because of what God accomplished in Jesus and the work of redemption for the entire world).*

Why is there **NOW no condemnation,** *even towards the world?*

I mean what attracts God to them?

Their sudden new behavior change and new conduct?

...Or is it what He achieved in Christ *when He was wounded by and for their transgressions and bruised by and for their iniquity?*

In His death and resurrection **He brought an end to all condemnation!**

For them and for us! *For all men anywhere and everywhere on the globe! For all of mankind, throughout all of time!*

Listen, **there is now THEREFORE no condemnation!**

And brethren, if you still teach that there still is some kind of condemnation and some kind of conditional statement there in Romans Eight verse One, *then brethren **you are not preaching the truth of the gospel!***

If you are still making salvation conditional and saying, *"Oh, it is only for those who are **IN** Christ Jesus, it only applies to you **IF** you are in Christ Jesus,"* **then you are not busy with the gospel *and you are preaching another message; something other than the gospel!***

If you still see salvation as something conditional **then you haven't even heard the gospel yet, *or you simply haven't understood it correctly,*** because we are all in Christ Jesus **whether you believe it or not.**

God already put you in Christ Jesus, way before you were even born, whether you believe it or not and whether you understand it yet or not!

1 Corinthians 1:30, *"Of God are you in Christ…"*

Listen, God identified the whole fallen world in His Son's death!

Hallelujah!

*"There is **now no condemnation**…"*

The ministry under the Law, the ministry of death, *that ministry of condemnation **no longer exists!***

And yes, I can say that with the utmost confidence *in the light of what God revealed and achieved in Christ on Man's behalf!*

Romans 8:2, *"**For** (because) the Law of the Spirit, that Law of Life in Christ Jesus…"*

What is the Law of the Spirit all about?

Life in union with Christ Jesus. ***Walking conscious of my oneness with Him.***

*"**For** (because) the Law of the Spirit of life in Christ Jesus **has set me free from the Law of Sin and Death**…"*

The Law of Sin and Death was the government of Sin that caused me to be a slave of sin. I expound on that more fully in my books *Resurrection Life Now* and *Zoë,* as well as in my book series or, Study Course: *The Gospel in 3-D!.*

Now Verse 3 of Romans 8 says,

*"**For God has done** what the Law (the Law of Moses) weakened by the flesh could not do. Sending His own Son in the likeness of sinful flesh, and as an offering (a gift), to deal with Sin; He condemned Sin in the flesh."*

It was a death blow to Sin! It officially spelled the end of Sin's reign over Man! It successfully brought Sin's reign to an end!

"And so the just requirement of the Law was fulfilled in us…"

Hallelujah!

It was fulfilled **in us,** in our association with Christ Jesus, *not by us,* amen!

Can you see with me that that is the basis of God's faith, *and therefore the bases for your faith?*

God in Christ has set me free from everything that the Law was weak in doing.

Why was the Law weak in doing these things; *in setting me free?*

Because the ability and the strength of the law was measured by the ability, or should I rather say, the inability of the flesh to consistently keep (or do) the Law.

And so today, praise God, *we are a product of the liberty that the law of life in Christ Jesus, the law of faith has worked in us, amen.*

We are referring to the obedience **of** faith; to **faith-inspired** obedience.

I remind you just quickly of what Paul said way back there in Romans 1:5. He said that his mission through his ministry is to bring about **the obedience of faith,** for the sake of His name, among all the nations.

And in chapter 6:17 Paul says that *"thanks be to God that even though we were once slaves of sin, we have become **obedient from the heart** to the standard of teaching; (God's exact standard of teaching, revealed in Christ)."*

So in other words, what awakened that obedience? **The degree of revelation. The standard of teaching. The true gospel, amen!**

In Romans 10 Paul says,

"How will they believe?"

They will not believe *until they have heard, and understood accurately* amen.

He says in verse 17,

"So then, faith comes by hearing, and hearing comes by the word (by the word concerning Christ, by the gospel, by the good news, by the standard of teaching, by revelation into the work of redemption and what actually happened and how it practically affects us all).*"*

"So then, faith comes by hearing, and hearing by the revelation of Christ!"

That *"hearing"* Paul is talking about which produces understanding and produces faith, is not hearing by the Law again.

I say again; that *"hearing"* is not hearing the Law again, brethren, *it's hearing Christ, it's hearing the gospel!*

That's what awakens faith!

What kind of faith does it awaken?

It awakens the kind of faith *that views me in His opinion of me.*

And through that mixing together of truth and faith and love in my heart, *the energy of that word is released.*

Chapter 8

Walk In The Light As He Is

In 1 John 1, there in the first five verses, John speaks of a fellowship with Deity that is enjoyed in the light of God's approval given to us in Christ.

He says it is such a richness of fellowship where there is no trace of darkness. That means there is no trace of self-effort, because darkness speaks of self-effort, it speaks of the senses.

He describes a fellowship that is inspired by the Word that was from the beginning.

He says we have heard about it. In fact, we have heard enough to quicken a new perception. And what we have heard has become tangible evidence in our lives, a testimony.

And so he says that now, in the communicating of my testimony, in writing to you this letter, I desire for you to also hear enough to be included in that same KONONIA, in the same **intimate fellowship**, and surely our **fellowship** (around the truth; created by the truth) is an **intimate fellowship** with the Father and with His Son Jesus Christ, *and these* *things we now write to you, and make fully know to you,* **so that <u>your joy</u> may be full.**

And then there in 1 John 1:6 he speaks of the man who fails to appropriate this *because of self-deception.*

But now here in Verse 7 he says,

"But if we walk in the light **as He is in the light,** *we have* **fellowship** *with one another,"*

And what happens *spontaneously?*

A *cleansing* **takes place.**

"…the blood of Jesus **cleanses us** *from* **all unrighteousness.***"*

Do you see, I am not walking in the light of my sin. *I am walking in the light of His provision,* **and a spontaneous cleansing takes place!**

Of course it is only logical that if I am walking *in the light of* **deception,** *trying to hide my sin from the Lord and trying to make-believe as if I'm all right when I know I'm not, when I know everything is wrong,* **then I only deceive myself,** *so we are not talking about* **deceiving ourselves and preferring to continue in sin.** That is not what we are teaching!

You will never find us promoting self-deception and sin!

...BUT I want you to get this point, and remember it clearly that <u>walking in the light does not mean, walking in the light of your sin</u>.

Jesus says in John 8, *"If you continue in my word, you shall know the truth and the truth shall set you free!"*

Just recently, I turned on the television and heard a professor of religion teach that you must know the truth of the problem. And then he proceeded for the next hour to tell of one problem after another that he encounters in his practice, and the one problem is worse than the other and even uglier, and you left that show feeling dirty, *and that was now somehow supposed to help and encourage us.*

Jesus did not say that you will know the truth of the problem. *No, He said that you will know the truth of His provision **and that is what will liberate you!***

So walking **in the light** has nothing to do with, *'Oh, brother, we've got this problem between us, you and I, so let's get in the light with it, let's speak it out into the open and let's speak our minds and be frank with one another, and talk freely and openly about it and cut one another down to size, and humiliate one another, and let's get into the light with our problem.'*

Listen, you'll just get into deeper bondage that way. *I've not yet seen any **real reconciliation** take place based upon that.*

I've only ever seen more hurt and devastation and masks and hypocrisy come from it *because it is not a principle of the Word.*

Walking in the light means to escape into the revelation of what His grace reveals concerning all of us.

In the light of what grace reveals we can no longer afford to see each other after the flesh. We can no longer see any man from a human point of view.

We escape that old point of view, that old mindset by putting on the new. We escape into the revelation of His grace and His abundance on our behalf. And as we escape into that, there is a new demand that we place upon Him, His resources, and a new way of interacting with one another.

Not a demand to perform, but a demand within ourselves to embrace the truth as the truth; to embrace our original design restored to us in Jesus Christ, and to embrace one another truly in love, to embrace one another as loved-ones and fellow heirs of the grace of life!

You see, as we embrace the truth as the truth within ourselves we automatically challenge and quicken the same kind of response in others towards us in return. And even if it is not reciprocated, it doesn't matter, it doesn't change our focus in the Spirit, or our demand upon God's resources, because for us, the truth remains the truth, and it now completely governs me as well as my responses and my conduct!

You see, if you're in conflict with another person and you place a demand on that person's conduct to change, or you place a demand on that person's behavior to adjust itself *before you are going to continue to extend your approval of them and to them,* you put that person back under the law as well as back into bondage, amen.

And you know what you are then really doing? You are ministering condemnation and death.

I guarantee that if we place a demand upon one another in terms of only one thing: *the full knowledge and acknowledgment of the nature of God that indwells us all,* then my confidence is not in your conduct my brother, or sister, *but it's in the nature of Him that has come to abide in you, and that nature is quickened by me walking in the light, and by me and you both together now, walking in that same light, as He is in the light.*

And so if I put any kind of demand upon your life, it will be a demand upon that nature; **awakening and enlarging your revelation of it,** no longer regarding you with suspicion from a human point of view, but regarding you **only in terms of His excellent approval of you.**

And you see there is enough wealth in His love awakened in our hearts **for us to prevail in unity, to prevail in absolute oneness,** *as we together believe in one another, and believe in God's working within our hearts, through the truth and through His love continually reinforced ...and so, we cannot help but anticipate His best in one another, without any* *fleshly expectation or disappointment attached to it.*

That's what walking in the light **as He is in the light** is all about!

Hallelujah!

Listen, I want to inspire your obedience of faith afresh and anew, as you discover Him afresh and anew as your Alpha and Omega in this book. Don't interrupt *His beginning* with your own effort. Don't let that which was begun in your life *through hearing with faith* to be interrupted through the works of the law.

Continue in a consciousness of His indwelling and of His investment in you. Continue that consciousness within yourself and towards one another, *continue that ongoing conversation, that fellowship,* and you will discover a prevailing in these things, a whole new kind of forbearing, a strength of forbearing with one another, and an anticipating of His best in one another, *manifesting to the full.*

This can be clearly seen through what Jesus instructed, and through what we have *in the prophetic picture of the bread and wine.*

Listen, God wants us to take a fresh hold of a covenant that He initiated and that He fulfilled *as we embrace His love together in friendship with one another, and in sweet fellowship.*

And as we do that, as we partake of this eternal love covenant together, this joyous celebration of eternal life, life more abundantly, life, and that in abundance, He wants us to discover that we have eaten together of the bread from above that did not come to satisfy us for a moment and leave us hungry again, starving again, having to hypocritically seek glory and affection again tomorrow.

See, every time we come together in friendship and fellowship in the light as He is in the light, and share a meal together, God wants us to do it in the light of Philemon 1:6.

Every time we get together and sit down and share an intimate meal together in friendship and fellowship *around the gospel, around redemption truth and redemption reality, with Jesus as the topic and center of our conversation,* **acutely aware of our oneness with Him, because of what He has done,** *then we will discover that even our food prophesies to us of that* **oneness** *and declares that* **oneness.**

Our meal together, our fellowship together, our love feast and even our very friendship because of it, is *a communication, an ongoing conversation,* **a declaring of our faith; of our persuasion in His unchanging love for us and indeed for all people everywhere!**

The RSV translation of that verse says that the communication or the declaring of our faith **must promote the knowledge of every good thing** *that is already within us* **in Christ.**

And then also in 2 Corinthians 13 Paul says that if you examine yourself, if you test yourself, discover one thing and one thing only: *Christ's indwelling* – **Christ indwelling you to the full!**

Hey, this is not a cop-out for your own failure, but a release *from* your failure, because His indwelling, the fullness of it, is the very thing, the very knowledge *that activates your faith* **perfecting the work of grace in your life.**

Father we bow our hearts to you today. We thank you for our daily bread and for our daily cup, and we thank you that as we are partaking of that bread and of that cup it prophesies to us: *it speaks and declares to us of our partaking of Christ and our* **oneness** *with Him.*

We thank you Father that as we are reminded even in our food, and as we then also daily partake of Christ, we are sealing the testimony of God, the faith of God, in our hearts, through that tangible contact and communion and oneness that You have awakened in us, and that we then now also mirror back to You, and that we then also reflect to one another, *as we partake of Your grace,* **united together in Christ Jesus in friendship and fellowship with You and with one another,** *as a people full of faith;* **as Your own special people.**

Thank you, Father, that there is therefore **now no condemnation!** Thank you, Father, that we have confidence, by the blood of Jesus **to**

come freely into the freedom of this place where You are, where You exist.

Thank you that we stand **blameless** in this place. We are standing **innocent** by the new and living way *which You have prepared for us as a gift.*

Jesus, thank you that we have indeed an unreserved approach, to stand before our Father, and so we enter into that holy place where You are right now, Father, with boldness, with a new confidence, and we come to worship You with all our hearts for who You are.

Father, we give You praise and we worship You. You are indeed the Creator of the earth and You are El Shaddai, the God of plenty, the All Sufficient One, and You are indeed our Father God, the Holy One who gave our spirits birth!

So we adore You, and we give You glory, and we lift on high Your holy name!

Our Father God, we worship You, You are the Most High God from whom we came!

Right now, we worship you for who You are, our Father God, our Daddy, our Papa, *the One who has been in love with us from before time began, and who has also come, in time, to win back our hearts in love,* ***through Your own immense love for us which You demonstrated in Christ Jesus!***

Thank you Father for this knowledge!

Thank you that we have indeed come to know and love You for who You are, *for we do know and believe the love You have for us.*

Amen.

If you have never encountered God personally, then I believe you just have in the pages of this book as you have read the content of what I have just said.

If you have started reading this book as a stranger to God, be assured that you no longer are. **You are not a stranger to Him; you are fully embraced and welcomed by Him.**

In this book **He has extended His heart to you and He wants you to know that He has fully welcomed and embraced you into His family already,** *through His Son Jesus Christ...*

*...All you have to do is **accept it as so** and simply **be** reconciled to Him in your heart. You can begin a relationship with Him **right now,** all you have to do is **embrace Him; embrace His friendship.***

Listen, do not be deceived by man-made religion. Do not be deceived in partaking of communion merely in a religious manner. True communion with Him cannot be reduced to a mere ritual; to a few crackers or, wafers, and some fake wine or grape juice of some sort; not even if it includes real wine; it cannot replace or become a substitute for real communion and fellowship in the truth of the Gospel and the oneness with Him it produces!

Holy Communion, intimate communion, that constant friendship and fellowship with God, as Daddy, as Papa; our **oneness with Him,** *cannot be reduced to a mere religious ritual or even some short little morning devotion.*

Either He becomes your **constant companion in life, your lover,** and your friendship and fellowship constantly **grows richer and fuller** over time, *or you do not really know Him in the way He wants to be known by you.*

Having a relationship with God was never meant to be a casual friendship or a religious ritual kind of thing.

It's meant to be a companionship, a vibrant ongoing constant love affair and intimate fellowship…

…After all, **He is love**, and He is the ever present living God, your true Father, your Daddy, your Papa, *who loves you dearly!*

He loves you immensely!

Today He wants you to partake, by faith, of the bread, of the food, of the truth of redemption, in covenant relationship with Him and with His Son: that means, *simply embrace your redemption fully!*

Embrace what Jesus did as a reality!

Embrace your reconciliation with Father God as a reality!

Embrace His forgiveness and His friendship and His fellowship as a reality!

Embrace His love!

Embrace Him now as the only One who really loves you!

Embrace that love-relationship fully and enter into it!

If you don't know how to start, open up your heart to Him and simply begin a conversation with Him, expressing whatever is on your heart!

He hears and He knows and He understands.

All He has ever wanted to do was to embrace you and love you!

Come on, let us just together be overwhelmed again with the fact that His body was torn on our behalf. **His body was torn on *your* behalf!**

It was torn to break through the veil of our indifference and our independence and our unbelief so that now we can draw near again as it was before the fall of Man **so that we can now draw near again with confidence** *through understanding His love for us displayed in the broken body of Jesus.*

I want to encourage you, right there where you sit reading this book, right now, draw near in your heart to God, *with a new confidence.*

In your heart, *embrace your covenant with Him and enjoy the wealth of His love that is yours always.*

Hey, you have His full attention and affection, *now give Him yours!*

Everything that belongs to you, everything concerning God that is already yours in Christ Jesus, **possess it fully!**

Lay a hold of it in your faith *today.*

And then also recognize that you are in co-covenant together with the rest of us here on planet earth.

You are in co-covenant of these things with your family and your neighbors, even your enemies, amen.

And as you realize and recognize these things, then simply become a minister of these things to your family and your neighbors.

Share this book with them.

Get my books on *God's Love for You* and *God's Inheritance in You* and perhaps also my book called: *Fully Persuaded,* and share it with as many of your friends as possible.

Go ahead and share it with strangers too, even your enemies, and watch God, by His love, do the same work in their hearts as He has begun in yours.

In closing, I urge you to get yourself a copy of the Mirror Study Bible, it is the best paraphrase translation of the Scriptures from the original Greek that I have ever read, and it's available online at Barnes & Noble and several other book sellers.

If you want me or someone a part of our team to come to where you are, *anywhere in the world,* and give a talk or teach you and some of your friends *about the gospel message and these redemption realities,* simply contact us at www.livingwordintl.com …or you can always find me on www.facebook.com

If your life has changed as a result of reading this book, *please write to me and let me know.*

I would love to share in your joy,

…so that my joy in writing this book may be full!

"That which was from the beginning,

which we have heard
(with our spiritual ears),
which we have seen
(with our spiritual eyes),
which we have looked upon
(beheld, focused our attention upon),
and which our hands have also handled
(which we have also experienced),

concerning the Word of life,

we declare to you,

that you also may have this
fellowship with us;

and truly our fellowship is with
the Father
and with His Son Jesus Christ.

And these things we write to you
that your joy may be full.
                    ~ 1John 1:1~4

About the Author

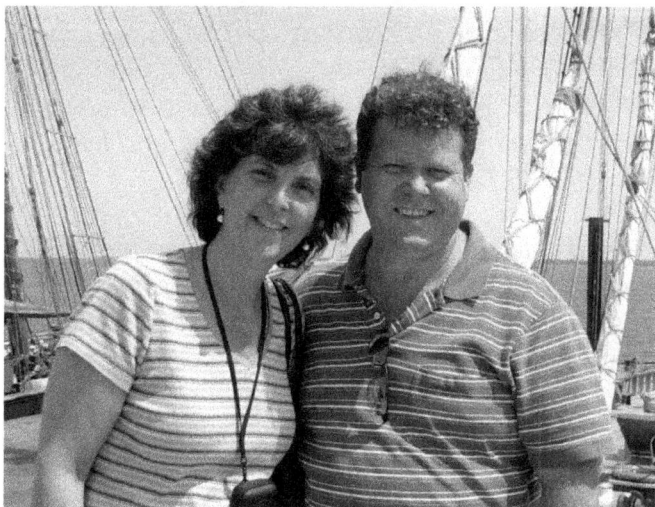

Rudi & Carmen Louw together oversee: Living Word International.

They also travel and minister both locally and internationally.

Rudi was born and raised in the country of South Africa, while Carmen grew up in Cortland, New York.

They function in the ministry of reconciliation (2 Corinthians 5:18-21) and flow strongly with the Holy Spirit and His anointing to teach, preach, prophesy, heal, and whatever is needed to touch people's lives with the reality of God's love and power.

God has given them keen insight into what He has to say to mankind in the work of redemption concerning the revelation and restoration of humanity's true identity.

Therefore they emphasize THE GOSPEL, IN CHRIST REALITIES, the GRACE of God, the WORD OF RIGHTEOUSNESS, *and all such eternal truths essential to salvation and living the CHRIST-LIFE.*

They have been granted this wisdom and revelation into the knowledge of God by the resurrected Spirit of Jesus Christ, *to establish and strengthen believers in the faith of God, and to activate them in ministering to others.*

Not only are people set free from the poison and bondage of sin, condemnation and all kinds of intimidation, (upheld, strengthened and reinforced by age old religious ideas born out of ignorance) **but many are brought into a closer more intimate relationship with Father God, as Daddy**, through accurate teaching and unveiling of the gospel message, prophetic words, healings and miracles.

Rudi & Carmen are closely knitted together with many other effective Christians, church fellowships, and groups of believers who share the same revelation and passion **to impart the truth of the gospel to others, so as to impact and transform the world we live in with the LOVE and POWER of God.**